SAUL OF TARSUS

A BIOGRAPHY OF THE APOSTLE PAUL

MATTHEW MURRAY

LifeCaps Biography Series
ANAHEIM, CALIFORNIA

Contents

About LifeCaps

LifeCaps is an imprint of BookCaps™ Study Guides. With each book, a lesser known or sometimes forgotten life is recapped.

We publish a wide array of topics (from baseball and music to literature and philosophy), so check our growing catalogue regularly (www.bookcaps.com) to see our newest books.

THE SOURCES FOR PAUL'S LIFE

For any biography, one gathers the available sources and builds a life story based on these varied sources. Each source is incomplete, serving its own purpose having been written for a specific reason. Sources can also be multilayered with one biographer using an-

other, who in turned may have used birth cer-
tificates, press releases, journal entries from
family members, or interviews from family and
friends to obtain biographical information.
Each source must be weighed for its value and
some sources flatly contradict others.

This situation becomes especially dicey
when dealing with religious figures. For some
believing communities, historically evaluating
religious documents, like the New Testament,
is tantamount to blasphemy. On the other
hand, devout Christian scholars from the very
beginnings of the church have engaged in this
type of critical study of the New Testament
while active members within the Christian
church.

The primary, most authoritative source
available for information about Paul is contained in the many long letters that he wrote to
congregations and individuals throughout the
Roman Empire. These letters contain auto-
biographical references, but also reveal his level of education and his style of speech. Scholars have given priority to the letters of Paul
over the material contained in the book of

4 | *Saul of Tarsus*

Acts, since John Knox made his famous argument on the subject in 1946.

There are several letters that appear in the New Testament attributed to Paul that by virtue of style, content or both are not considered authentic Pauline epistles. These letters are called Deutero-Pauline and include Ephesians, Colossians and II Thessalonians, but scholars still dispute the authenticity of these letters. The group of letters called the Pastorals that include I and II Timothy and Titus are much more widely recognized as not authentic Pauline epistles. These latter address church polity issues that come up decades after Paul lived.

The Acts of the Apostles, generally referred to simply as the book of Acts was the second book that Luke wrote for Theophilus as a two volume narrative account of Christianity from the birth of Jesus to the spread of Christianity to the center of the empire, Rome itself. Luke was an educated Greek writer who wrote in the tradition of Greek historians using a combination of written and oral sources that he fleshed out into a broader narrative with a running theme. Since Paul's missionary activity was one of the primary driving factors behind the spread of the gospel throughout the Roman Empire, Paul understandably plays a prominent role in Luke narrative. But it is abundantly clear that Luke was not as concerned with presenting factual information that double and triple checked for accuracy as much as he was in telling a compelling narrative about the miraculous spread of the gospel message throughout the region that would edify Theophilus and the other Christians with whom he would share these volumes.

One of the sources that Luke used appears in what are called the "we passages" of Acts. These passages seem to hold up fairly well to historical scrutiny and likely derive from a travel itinerary of one of Paul's travel companions. These sections are easily identified by readers of the book when Luke switches quite suddenly from describing the things that "they" did to describing the things that "we" did or that happened to Paul and "us." These passages in particular carry a terrific deal of weight in reconstructing the facts of Paul's life.

An early Christian scholar, Clement of Alexandria contains some information about Paul's death hat is not contained in the New Testament and appears to be based on reliable oral tradition as were many of the passages in Acts. Another second century document called the Acts of Paul relates more oral tradition about the apostle. It is not canonical or considered inspired by the Christian church, but this does not mean that it does not contain some historical information that can be gleaned.

Caveats for Both Believers and Non-Believers

This biography is intended as a historical biography on the life of possibly the most influential Christian writer of the early church. It can be read profitably by both believers and non-believers but at some points has the potential to offend both groups. Paul was a religious figure, and as such he had religious experiences that he believed were divine encounters. These experiences, when considered historically reliable, are presented as genuine without critique or criticism. Believers and non-believers should both be able to read about these experiences from their own perspective without difficulty. Believers can easily view them as genuine events and divine encounters. Non-believers, in turn, can easily view them as experiences that Paul or his companions attributed to the divine realm because of their worldview, but which can be explained from psychological or sociological perspectives.

A case in point appears in Paul's visit to Philippi where he interacts with a slave-girl. Luke relates first part of the story as follows:

And it came to pass, as we were going to the place of prayer, that a certain maid having a spirit of divination met us, who brought her masters much gain by soothsaying. The same following after Paul and us cried out, saying, These men are servants of the Most High God, who proclaim unto you the way of salvation. And this she did for many days. But Paul, being sore troubled, turned and said to the spirit, I charge thee in the name of Jesus Christ to come out of her. And it came out that very hour. (Acts 16:16-18)

This belongs to one of the "we passages" in Acts and there should be no reason to dismiss this event on historical grounds as legendary as Koester does (cf. Koester, Introduction to the New Testament, vol. 2 p. 108). There is no reason to think that this entry does not derive from a legitimate travel diary of one of Paul's companions. Believers and non-believers alike can both readily agree with this conclusion. But just because the event is historically reliable, says nothing about whether it is phenomenologically reliable. Paul and his companion writing the diary clearly believed that the slave-girl had been possessed by a demon and that Paul drove the demon out of the girl. Contemporary Greek sources abound with similar stories about exorcism in multiple religious contexts. Believing the event occurred historically and holding specific beliefs about the nature of that event are two different things.

Luke then shifts gears and switches back to his own voice as he describes the aftermath of this event. It seems clear from a literary historical perspective that Luke had before him a source that told about the exorcism and Paul's references in his letters that talked about being persecuted in the city. In an effort to make a compelling and continuous narrative Luke embellished the story with information about the impact of this act on the girl's handlers connecting this event with Paul's persecution in that city. As such, the embellishment falls into the category of Christian legend. Nonbelievers will have no problem dismissing this as legendary. Believers, on the other hand, are often quite squeamish about allowing a place for legendary material within the authoritative canon of the church. Prominent Christian theologians and scholars have had little difficulty making such pronouncements while at the same time affirming the inspiration, edification and authority of these same books since the inception of the Christian church.

[1]

PAUL'S EARLY LIFE

Paul was born to middle-class Jewish parents in a Jewish home in Tarsus, which lies about ten miles north of the Mediterranean Sea. He grew up speaking Greek and learned Torah from the Septuagint, the Greek translation of the Old Testament.

He was circumcised when he was eight days old and likely attended synagogue with his parents on a regular basis. His parents gave him the Hebrew (Jewish) name Saul, but also gave him a Roman name, Paul. At home, in the synagogues and with fellow Jews he would have used the name Saul, but in all other circumstances he would have used his Roman name, Paul.

As a boy of seven to eight years old, Paul was likely taught reading, writing and basic math by his father. Saul never became comfortable writing his own letters, and when he did write, it was with large letters, like those children tend to make (Gal. 6:11). After that point, his education would have been conducted at the synagogue, where he would learn Torah and the interpretive traditions of the Rabbis. If Paul did speak Hebrew or Aramaic, this would have been the context where he received that instruction. The city of Tarsus was home to several prominent Stoic philosophers, and one of Saul's teachers had likely been trained in one of the Stoic schools. It is clear that certain aspects of this Stoic thought were taught to Saul in a somewhat diluted form. His parents likely supplemented his synagogue education with a private tutor. Even though his family was not upper class, education was highly valued in Tarsus. This private tutor is the one who would have taught Paul the canons of rhetoric that Paul uses throughout his theological arguments in his letters. This tutor is also the source from which Paul would have learned Greek poetry, like that of Menander, who he quotes in his first letter to the Corinthians (1 Cor. 15:33).

Around the age of fourteen or fifteen, his father would have then begun to teach Paul about the fine art of tent making, bringing him alongside as an apprentice. In addition to its Stoic philosophers, the city of Tarsus was renowned for its high quality tents. From his father, he learned the craft of using cilicium, a strong wool made of goat's hair, to make tents.

It is essential to highlight a discrepancy between the biographical sketch of Paul's early life laid out above and the information provided by Luke. Luke quotes Paul as saying "I am a Jew, born in Tarsus in Cilicia, but brought up in this city [Jerusalem] at the feet of Gamaliel..." (Acts 22:3). There are several reasons to suspect that Luke was using a little bit of poetic license in this instance. Paul makes no mention of his having a personal connection with Jerusalem or with Gamaliel in his own autobio-

graphical sketches (Phil. 3:5). Tradition records
Gamaliel as having a fairly tolerant attitude toward Christianity. Gamaliel also belonged to
the Jewish interpretive school (of Hillel) that
believed that a man could divorce his wife for
the simplest of reasons. Paul's outright hostility towards Christians and his views about marriage and divorce seem so diametrically
opposed to the views of Gamaliel that it is hard
to imagine that Paul was one of his students.
Finally, this information fits Luke's literary
scheme quite nicely by further portraying Paul
as very Jewish and would be the type of poetic
license one would expect for Luke to take
(Bornkamm, Paul, p. 3.). The reason Luke
would choose Gamaliel as the Rabbi with whom
Paul studied was his position with regard to
Gentiles. Gamaliel was known for his belief
that Gentiles should be actively converted to
the Jewish faith

There is also a fairly detailed description of
Paul's appearance contained in the Acts of Paul
and Thecla. It is probably more legend than
reality but is intriguing nonetheless. Titus
wrote a description of Paul for Onesiphorus,

who was to meet him in Iconium, but had not previously met him. Titus' description reads as follows: "a man small in size, bald-headed, bandy legged, of noble mien, with eyebrows meeting, rather hook-nosed…" (Acts of Paul and Thecla 1:3).

[2]

EARLY CAREER (PRE-CONVERSION)

When Paul finished his apprenticeship with his father, he set out from Tarsus to Damascus, where he could make a name for himself as a tent maker. He found lodging and connected with the local synagogue. It was in Damascus that Paul seems to have established himself as both a craftsman and a Pharisee.

It was likely here in Damascus around 32 CE that Paul took his Nazarite vow for a period of twenty years. During the next twenty years, he would be bound by this vow and could not drink wine nor could he shave or cut his hair. Although there is only a brief mention in Acts (18:18) about the ritual conclusion of this vow, there are no sources that indicate when it was taken. Such a vow would seem out of character after Paul's conversion given his views on the law, but this type of vow would be entirely expected during his life as zealous Jew and Pharisee. The Mishnah dictates that the period specified for a Nazirite vow could not be less than thirty days (Nazir ix 5). For Paul to make a vow for twenty years seems like an exceptionally long time, but the Pharisees with whom Paul associated likely took pride in the extended length of time associated with their vows.

It was in this context then that he began "persecuting" Jewish Christians. He talked closely with the members of his synagogue, and when he discovered that a member had accepted the Hellenistic version of Christianity that taught Christians were free from the obligations of the law, he excluded them from the synagogue community. Because these Jewish Christians no longer obeyed the commandments set out in the Torah, they were no longer welcome as Jews. Paul may have also scourged these Jewish Christians, which was a punishment that the Roman authorities allowed to synagogues.

This movement and its adherents incensed Paul so much because they attempted to persuade other members of the synagogue congregation to their views and in so doing, they were undermining the authority of the Torah, the very heart of the Jewish religion. For this reason, Paul may have also brought such synagogue members before the local courts in Damascus and even before the Roman authorities. It is likely doing to these Christians the same types of things that would be later done to him, by Jewish leaders in various cities where he preached. The case in Corinth is a good example where the Jewish authorities brought Paul before the Roman proconsul, Gallio. They made their case to Gallio, but he dismissed it as a matter of religious doctrine and sent it back to the Jewish leaders (Acts 18:12-17). Until the time of Nero, the only times when the Roman authorities took particular notice of the Christians was when the Jewish authorities were able to accuse them of some crime against the state, like when the Jewish leaders in Thessalonica were able to claim treason for claiming Jesus to be a king (Acts 17:1-9). So while this option would have been open to Paul, as well, even if he used it occasionally, he likely never got much traction with this line of persecution.

Luke's portrayal of this period of Paul's life in the book of Acts contains several elements that strain credulity. According to Luke, Paul persecuted Christians directly by walking about with letters from the high priest that gave him the authority to bring Christians from outside Palestine to Jerusalem for punishment. Luke also has Paul dragging Christians from their houses and throwing them into prison. But the Roman government never extended any such authority to the Sanhedrin nor to the high priest. For Luke's narrative, it was crucial to paint Paul as the arch-villain prior to his call. He wanted his Christian readers to connect on an emotional level with the fear that many of the Jewish Christians who met Paul shortly af-ter his call felt. The darker the hat Luke could situate on Paul, the more powerful would appear the message of Christ that had changed him so dramatically.

[3]

CONVERSION AND MINISTRY

While Paul was living in Damascus, around 35 CE, he had a personal experience where he encountered the risen Christ. This experience was one that would mark Paul's life from that moment forward. Luke focuses on the nature of the vision Paul had and the identity of the figure that appeared to Paul. Luke separates Paul's vision of Christ when he was called by him to be an apostle to the Gentiles that Luke sets in Jerusalem from Paul's initial vision of Christ that occurred in Damascus.

But when Paul describes his experience with the risen Christ, he emphasizes that it was this revelation experience where he was called as an apostle to the Gentiles. He also emphasizes that he was divinely taught the message of the gospel and that he had no human mentor in the faith (Gal. 1:1, 11-12). Once Christ had revealed himself to Paul, he told no one else of this experience, but presumably continued to Damascus where he immediately packed his bags and set off to Arabia for a period of religious self-reflection (Gal. 1:15-17). The way that Paul describes it, this was not a period of missionary activity or some type of Christian apprenticeship, but was a solitary period in his life (Gal. 1:15-17). This is where Paul learned the Christian faith—in solitude in Arabia with only himself and Jesus (Gal. 1:11-17). He came out of that experience convinced that Jesus was both Lord (κυριος) (1 Cor. 9:1; Phil. 3:8) and the Son of God (ὑιος του θεου) (Gal. 1:16).

Luke's references to Paul's blindness and his companions on the road, and to Ananias all seem to be in stark contradiction to Paul's own statements about this event. Each of these elements serves the literary purposes of Luke and can be considered poetic license. The blindness and involuntary fast aided with the suspense of the story and the figure of Ananias helped to confer prophetic sanctioning of Paul and his ministry.

Having been active as a Pharisee, it took Paul some time to work out the implications of the risen Christ for his relationship to the Torah, translated into Greek as 'the law'. The gospel message that Paul received from the risen Christ meant the end of the validity of the law and the dawning of a new requirement for God's people, which was to be 'in Christ'. It was in Arabia that he reconciled himself to an itinerant lifestyle, knowing that he take his tradecraft with him as spread the message of the gospel to the Gentiles. It was only after Paul believed that he had a firm grasp on the Christian faith and his mission to the Gentiles that he returned to Damascus, presumably to wrap up his affairs with his business and his lodging there. He was also baptized in Damascus and may have spent some time in reconciliation with those Christians in Damascus whom he had persecuted.

Once Paul had concluded his affairs in Damascus he then traveled to Jerusalem to meet with the leaders of the Christian movement, Peter and James (Gal. 1:18). He remained in Jerusalem for two weeks, where he likely discussed his plans to spread the Christian message to the Gentile world (Gal. 1:18). At this time, it seems that he did go into much detail with Peter and James about the specifics of the gospel that he had received from Jesus. He likely referred to the term 'gospel' without either of them defining what they meant by the term. With these vague descriptions, Peter and James appear to have given their assent to Paul's missionary aspirations.

It should not come as that much of a surprise that Paul chose his hometown of Tarsus in Cilicia as the first region where he would spread the gospel message (Gal. 1:21). Peter and James apparently informed Barnabus about their visit with Paul and his mission to the Gentiles. Barnabus was based in Antioch, and when he heard about Paul's goals, he believed hey coincided closely with his own. He, therefore, went to Tarsus to find Paul and ask him to join him in his work in Antioch. Paul likely saw the work in Antioch, the capital of Syria, as a logical extension of the work he had been doing in Cilicia. There Paul joined Barnabus and several other 'prophets and teachers' in Antioch mentioned in the credible list that Luke gives in Acts 13:1 that likely goes back to a reliable written source. Paul and Barnabus then spent several years preaching and evangelizing together in Antioch. Paul informs his readers that the total time he spent in Cilicia (Tarsus) and Syria (Antioch) was ten years, but there is no way to know how this time was divided between the two locations.

Paul and Barnabus had thought that things were going smoothly in Antioch. Paul had already met with Peter and James in Jerusalem and had received their blessing for his Gentile mission. He had developed good report with Barnabus, his coworker, and the church was growing. Then some Aramaic-speaking Jewish Christians had moved from Jerusalem to Antioch and had joined the congregation. These

Jewish Christians, who had been taught the 'gospel' message by Peter and James were aghast at how the 'gospel' message was being taught by Paul and Barnabus. As far as they had been taught, being a Christian was synonymous with being a Jewish Christian—the two went hand in hand. To make matters worse, these Jewish Christians were able to undermine Paul and Barnabus' authority by noting that they had been taught the 'gospel' by apostles who had been disciples of Jesus, and thereby carried more weight than did Paul. It was unthinkable to these Jewish Christians that one could be a Christian without being circumcised. It was only at this point that Paul realized his oversight. He had talked with Peter and James at length about bringing the 'gospel' to the Gentiles, but neither of them had clearly defined what it was they meant by the term 'gospel'.

The martyrdom of Stephen reported by Luke had been part of a defining moment in the Jerusalem church, when the Jews expelled the Christian Hellenists from Jerusalem because they taught that the laws of Moses were no longer binding. It was these Hellenistic Christians who appeared in Damascus that Paul had been bent on persecuting. This left the Jerusalem church filled with Aramaic-speaking, circumcised Jewish Christians who still obeyed the Mosaic Law. Peter and James, therefore, led a church that did not attempt to proselytize the Gentiles and expected Jesus' second coming to occur in Jerusalem in their lifetime. The Christian churches in the Diaspora, on the other hand, were made up of uncircumcised Greek-speaking Christians who had no prior connection to the law of Moses. The missionaries to these churches had not required their converts to accept circumcision or the law of Moses, but had instead built up a theological tradition that explained why in the aftermath of Jesus' death and resurrection such requirements were no longer necessary.

So some fourteen years after his initial call, in 48 CE, in an effort to ensure the unity of the church, Paul took Barnabus and Titus to Jerusalem. The risen Christ had provided him another revelation that the leaders of both facets of the church needed to clarify among themselves what they each meant by the term 'gospel' to ensure that there would be no lasting division between these two fundamental elements of the Christian church. This meeting is often considered the most momentous event in the history of the primitive church and Luke places it in the center of the book of Acts (ch. 15) dividing the church's work in Jerusalem from Paul's missionary activity to the Gentiles and Paul spends a considerable portion of his letter to the Galatians (2:1-10) discussing it.

At this council, behind closed doors, Peter clarified what he believed the gospel message entailed and Paul in turn shared his conception of the gospel message (Gal 2:2). The council listened to both leaders and did not exalt one above the other, a priori. After hearing their explanations, the council conferred and decided that both 'gospel' messages were consistent with the mission of the church, but were appropriate in two different sociological situations. The council endorsed Peter's role in the church as a missionary to the circumcised believers, while at the same time endorsing Paul's mission to the uncircumcised believers (Gal 2:7-

10). This decision of the council would prove to be problematic at a later time, but all parties left the council satisfied that the churches essential unity was intact.

Paul, Barnabus and Titus returned to Antioch and were able to clarify for their congregation the position of the Jerusalem leaders on these questions relating to the law of Moses and circumcision. Shortly after they returned, Peter visited them in Antioch, possibly as a planned follow-up to the Apostolic Council to ensure that the congregation had no doubt of the support from the Jerusalem church (Gal 2:11). Peter was more than willing to volunteer for this as he was preparing to embark on his own missionary journey. Having met with Paul twice now, it is possible he wanted a firsthand look at what lay in store for him in terms of missionary work. Paul and Barnabus welcomed him graciously to join their congregation and the communal meals in which the early church regularly engaged. Peter was pleased to catch a glimpse of all that was entailed in such missionary activity in the Diaspora region.

James remained in Jerusalem so that both prominent leaders were not absent at the same time, but he sent his messengers along a few days after Peter had left (Gal 2:12). These messengers may not have been directly in-volved in the Apostolic Council since it met be-hind closed doors. So while these messengers wanted to assure the Gentile believers that they supported Paul and his mission, they themselves were uncomfortable breaking the Jewish dietary laws that they kept so stringent-ly. These messengers from James had no problem joining the Gentile congregation for their times of worship and preaching, but they gently declined the offer to join in the pork roast dinner that was on the menu for the con-gregation's common meal (Gal. 2:12).

This put Peter in an awkward position. These were members of his congregation, whom he taught to obey the law of Moses as a part of their Christian tradition, and if he joined the Gentiles in their communal meal, he would come off as hypocritical. On the other hand, if he refused to eat with the Gentile Christians, this would undermine the support that they

were trying to show the congregation. He
opted for the latter as the least of the two
evils. To make matters even more awkward,
Barnabus himself, who had been preaching
alongside Paul and eating communal meals for
years with this congregation joined Peter in po-
litely refusing to dine with the congregation.
This infuriated Paul and he took Peter to task
openly about it (Gal. 2:14). Furthermore, it
caused such a row between Paul and Barnabus
that the two brothers parted ways and Paul left
Antioch for further missionary work without
Barnabus.

It was this event that pushed Paul's views on
the subject to an even more extreme position.
Paul came to the conclusion that circumcised
Jewish Christians wee those who especially
needed to recognize that justification could not
be attained by works of the law. It was likely
this event that led Paul to also reject any particular role that he once might have thought
Jerusalem would play in the second coming of
Christ.

From Antioch Paul travelled north to the
Central Highlands of Asia Minor to cities like

Ancyra, Pessinus and Gordion where he stayed and preached for several months founding several Christian communities there. These communities formed the churches of Galatia to whom Paul would later write the letter to the Galatians. Paul was quite sick for a time while he was there, but he later thanks them for the kindness they showed him during his illness.

After founding these Christian communities in Galatia, Paul went to the city of Alexandria. While he was there, he had a vision of a Macedonian man inviting him to preach the gospel in Macedonia. He was obedient to what he believed the vision was telling him and took a boat to Neapolis. From Neapolis, he travelled to Philippi, where he was able to establish a Christian community.

There, he met a female Jewish proselyte named Lydia, who worked as a merchant, whom he baptized (Acts 16:14). In gratitude, she allowed Paul and Silas to stay in her house while they were there (Acts 16:15). One day Paul performed an exorcism of a slave girl that got the two of them into trouble with the local Roman authorities (Acts 16:16). He was flogged and put in jail for a brief period, where Paul managed to convert the jailor, before they were forced to leave the city.

Paul and Silas then travelled from Philippi to Thessalonica. In Thessalonica Paul set up shop as a tent maker (1 Thess. 2:9). Paul's radical gospel did not go over well with the Jews in Thessalonica. They incited a mob to attack Paul and Silas, who took refuge in the house of Jason, one of the local Christians (Acts 17:5). The mob seized Jason and charged him as a coconspirator to treason when they handed him over to the Roman authorities (Acts 17:6-7). Jason made bail and was released without incident (Acts 17:9). Paul and Silas then left Thessalonica under cover of night (Acts 17:10). They made a brief stop in Beroea, but Paul was not there long enough to do much of anything (Acts 17:10-15).

Paul went from Beroea to Athens from whence he sent Timothy back to Thessalonica to complete the work of founding the Christian community that ended so prematurely (Acts 17:15; I Tim. 3:2). After Timothy left Athens,

Paul then continued on to his next stop, Corinth (Acts 18:1).

Luke has Paul preaching and making converts while he was in Athens, as well, which seems to contradict what Paul has to say about his time in the city (1 Thess. 3:1). Paul's reference to "being left alone" there is made specifically in the context of no longer having Christian followers to disciple. According to Luke's account, Paul made to significant converts in Athens, Dionysius, the Areopagite and a woman named Damaris. The reason why this conversion of only two individuals would have been significant for Luke's audience was that Dionysius, the Areopagite, was the first bishop of Athens according to a second century bishop of Corinth, Dionysius of Corinth, in his letter to the Athenians.

In addition, the lengthy speech that Luke has put into Paul's mouth is a masterly piece of Christian preaching but tells us much more about Luke's theology than about Paul's. When Paul talks of the natural knowledge of God that all people can see and understand, he then makes the conclusion that, as a result, everyone is guilty in God's eyes. But the speech in Acts 17 only references a time of ignorance that God has overlooked. The speech in Acts 17 is entirely devoid of any mention of the crucifixion, which played a central role in Paul's proclamation of the gospel.

Paul soon arrived in Corinth where he quickly met up with a fellow tent maker named Aquila (Acts 18:2-3). The two of them immediately hit it off, not only were they both tent makers and Jewish Christians, but both were new arrivals in the city with Aquila recently having come from Italy and Paul, originally from Tarsus and now from many stops in between (Acts 18:2). Aquila introduced him to his wife Priscila, and she opened up their home for him to stay with them during his time in Corinth (Acts 18:3). Paul graciously accepted this offer and stayed with the couple for a period of eighteen months (Acts 18:11).

It was in Corinth that Timothy returned from Thessalonica to bring word to Paul of the situation there. Timothy reported that despite Paul's abrupt departure under suspicious circumstances, the church was still loyal to Paul and unshaken in their newfound faith. They were concerned, however, that the second coming of Jesus that Paul had described to them in his preaching of the gospel as such an imminent event, was delayed (I Thess. 5:1-11). More disturbingly, between the time of Paul's rapid departure and Timothy's follow-up visit, some of their own baptized congregation had died. They wanted to know from Paul by way of Timothy whether these baptized believers had missed out on their expected salvation by dying before the second coming of Jesus.

Paul wrote the letter designated I Thessalonians in response to these concerns. Perhaps, before addressing this specific letter in detail, it would be helpful to introduce Greek letter writing in general and Paul's letters in particular. Ancient Greek letters, including those of Paul, had a set pattern or formula that they followed that included seven key elements:

- Name of Writer and Addressee
- Greeting (often one word)
- Thanks for Good Health of Addressee

- Main Body
  - Doctrinal Teaching (Paul only)
  - Advice on Christian Living (Paul only)
- Personal News and Greetings
- Note of Exhortation or Blessing
  (sometimes in Paul's own hand)
- Farewell (often one word)

Paul always used an amanuensis to whom he dictated his letters, aside from a few marginal notes that he would add with his own hand.

Returning to specifically to the letter to the Thessalonians, Paul assured them that their loved ones had not missed out on their salvation by having died beforehand and exhorted them to continue leading sober and upright lives (I Thess. 4:13-18). It seems that Paul toned down this apocalyptic aspect of his preaching in some of the later churches he founded.

The New Testament book entitled II Thessalonians contains: 1) a different style of Greek than appears in Paul's authentic letters; 2) contains two thanksgiving addresses (1:3-4; 2:13-15); and 3) a level of literarily dependency on I Thessalonians that is characteristic of a later writer, rather than the same author. In terms of content, the eschatological (end-times) message in II Thessalonians that emphasizes specific signs of the end stands in sharp contrast to the eschatological message presented by Paul in I Thessalonians. As such, many scholars regard II Thessalonians as a pseudonymous from a later Christian writer with eschatological concerns.

As Paul and Aquila were talking shop one day, Aquila got the perfect idea that the two should go into business together (Acts 18:3). Paul was, after all, trained by some of the best tent makers in the empire and being able to advertise Paul's Tarsian training would certainly draw more customers in. Paul was always eager to provide for himself and to not appear before his congregations with his hand out. Corinth was a vibrant metropolitan city, and the hub of much commercial trade so there would be no shortage of work for the two of them.

When Paul turned to his mission's work in the city, he developed a new strategy. Since the main opposition that he was receiving

came from the Jews in each of the cities he visited, not surprisingly because of what Paul
taught about the law of Moses, Paul took a
new tack. He first took his message to the
Jews in the synagogue, but most of them opposed him (Acts 18:5-6). In a gesture typical of
the Jewish prophets, and advocated by Jesus
himself to his apostles, Paul shook the dust off
his clothes and announced that he had done his
due diligence and from that moment on would
focus his attention on the Gentiles, which was
his true calling from the risen Christ (Acts 18:6).

While staying in Corinth Paul had another
vision assuring him of his safety and security in
this city (Acts 18:9-10). Paul continued to
preach and to build the Christian community at
Corinth. At one point, some of the Jewish
leaders, who had to this point had no luck in
taking any action against Paul within the synagogue because of Paul's close relationship with
its leader Crispus, tried to appeal to the Roman
authorities (Acts 18:8). They brought Paul before the Roman tribunal in the city, presided
over by the proconsul of the region, Gallio
(Acts 18:12). There they accused Paul of rab-

ble-rousing, but their claims were quickly dismissed as matters of religious dispute of no concern to the state. Gallio released Paul none the worse for wear and Paul continued with mission undisturbed (Acts 18:14-17).

This new strategy had worked fairly well for Paul and rather than having to leave prematurely, he was able to leave on his own terms when he believed that he had established a vibrant thriving Christian community. Before leaving Corinth, the twenty years he had allotted for his Nazirite vow had elapsed, and he went to Cenchrea, a small suburb of Corinth, to perform the ritual ceremony to complete this vow (Acts 18:18).

He planned to make Ephesus the next stop along his journey, and invited his new friend and coworker Aquila to come to Ephesus with him along with his wife so that the two might continue to market their tent making services together. Having only recently arrived in Ephesus themselves, Aquila and Priscila had no ties to Corinth other than the business, so they eagerly agreed to join Paul in Ephesus and would become travelling companions of Paul for some years to come.

Paul, accompanied by Aquila and Priscila, sailed from Corinth to Ephesus (Acts 18:18). He took the time to get Aquila and Priscila situated, finding lodging and setting up their tent making shop before he departed for a solo journey. This journey appears to have been filled with personal errands that the itinerant missionary had not had time to complete. He first sailed to Caesarea, which was the port nearest Jerusalem (Acts 18:22). Part of the requirements for completing the ritual that signified the end of the Nazirite vow was to burn the hair on the altar in Jerusalem. The rabbis had stipulated that if one was not in Jerusalem when their vow was complete that they were to save the hair and bring it to Jerusalem where it could be ritually burned. Paul seems to have considered this Nazirite vow a personal vow between him and God, which he was fulfilling because of his sworn oath, not because of a commitment to the Mosaic law.

From Jerusalem Paul went north to Antioch (Acts 18:22). This portion of his trip was likely not only to visit the Christian community he had helped establish there, but also to visit with Peter and Barnabus and to ensure that there was no longer any bad blood between the three of them. This trip appears to have been successful, for when the two are mentioned in later letters there is no trace of any lingering hostility or bitterness towards them. But it would also seem that Peter had his own agenda when he met with Paul, where he reminded Paul that he had yet to make any progress on his commitment that he made at the Jerusalem council to "remember the poor." Paul recognized that he had been neglectful in this area and resolved to make good on this commitment. With his personal errands completed, Paul headed back toward Ephesus, but made one more stop along the way in Galatia to check up on the disciples he had made in the region three years earlier (Gal. 4:13f.).

While Paul was busy running his personal errands, Aquila and Priscila were taking care of things in their new home in Ephesus. They were both captivated by the Christian preaching of a newcomer, named Apollo (Acts 18:24-

26). This Apollo had been fortunate enough to witness firsthand the ministry of Jesus, but was not associated with Jesus' disciples at the time, but was one of the disciples of John the Baptist (Acts 18:25). Apollo had been teaching the message about Jesus that he learned for some twenty years by the time he came to Ephesus. Aquila and Priscila were able to fill in for Apollo, some of the gaps that separated his message from the message of the gospel that Paul was spreading throughout the kingdom (Acts 18:26). Apollo was grateful and skillfully worked this new perspective into his preaching. Since they informed him that Paul would be conducting missionary work shortly in Ephesus, Apollo expressed his desire to visit Greece, inquiring was missionary work that could be done there (Acts 18:27). Aquila and Priscila immediately thought of their home church in Corinth, and they suggested that with Apollo's oratory and leadership skill that he might do well to head the church in Corinth (in Achaia) that they had established with Paul. Aquila and Priscila wrote a letter of introduction for Apollo that was customary for travelers to carry when they were going to a location they had never before visited (Acts 18:27).

Paul arrived back in Ephesus and began his usual habit of familiarizing himself with whatever Christian community already existed in Ephesus (Acts 19:1). As he talked with various different believers in Ephesus, he found the influence of Apollo and the Johannine gospel that he preached rampant throughout the city. He was talking with them and asking them various questions about the key elements of the faith. When he made his way to the doctrine of the Holy Spirit, the Christians with whom he was speaking had never even heard of the Holy Spirit (Acts 19:2). He encountered a dozen believers who had heard the gospel from Apollo that gave him this same reaction (Acts 19:2-7). Because the traditional Trinitarian baptismal formula (Matt. 28:19) had not been used during their baptism, Paul rebaptized these dozen Ephesian believers using the Trinitarian formula that still exists in the church to this day.

Paul then used the same model that had worked so well in Corinth. He addressed the Jews with the message of the gospel only briefly for a period of three months. From that point on, he believed he had done his due diligence with the Jews in the city who hardened their hearts to his message, and he focused again on his true calling, the Gentiles. Those few Jews whom he had converted, Paul invited to leave the synagogue, and they now met at the school of Tyrannus entirely separated from the Jewish synagogue that had landed him in trouble in so many other cities previously. This school of Tyrannus (most likely the nickname the students gave him meaning "tyrant") was likely a lecture hall, where this philosopher or educator lectured in the cool hours of the morning, but was willing to rent the space to the Christian church during the heat of the day (Stott, The Message of Acts, pp. 305-6). Once , the mission in Ephesus was well-established, he sent Timothy to Corinth, most likely with his first letter to them, referred to in the letter designated I Corinthians (5:9), which was, unfortunately, not preserved by the church. During this period, he also met the slave Onesimus, who had run away from his master Philemon, in Colossae. He was surprised to see

Onesimus, because Paul had a close relationship with Philemon, having converted him a few years prior (Philemon 19). Onesimus heard Paul preaching the gospel and had become a Christian himself (Philemon 16). He had also made himself quite useful to Paul and to the mission in general.

It was in Ephesus that Paul wrote the majority of his letters to the churches. It is likely that he wrote his letter to the Galatians from Ephesus which is what later tradition asserts, but the date when Paul wrote this letter is one of the most difficult to pen down (Kee, Understanding the New Testament, p. 226). It is unclear how Paul heard about the trouble to which he so vociferously responds in his letter. He makes no reference to a letter that he received from the Galatians outlining the problems or to a coworker who has delivered him this bad news.

By whatever means he acquired the information, he learned that some Jewish Christian missionaries from the church in Jerusalem had appeared in the region of Galatia and were undermining Paul's authority. They were claiming that because they were taught by James (or perhaps Peter), the disciple of Jesus, they knew the true gospel message, and they wanted to correct the errors that Paul had taught them about the Christian faith. The specific errors that they had identified were that Gentile Christians did not have to be circumcised in order to be Christians and that they did not have to submit to the Torah.

Paul went ballistic. The amount of emotion behind the letter to the Galatians is almost palpable. In the usual position where on would expect Paul to thank God for the Galatians, he says instead, "I marvel that ye are so quickly removing from him that called you..." (Gal. 1:6). He then resorts to calling them names, "O foolish Galatians, who did bewitch you..." (Gal. 3:1). Toward the end of the letter, he even gives voice to a wish that the knife would slip in his opponents' hands so that instead of just cutting the foreskin off that they would lop off their own genitals entirely (Gal. 5:12).

He first reasserts his authority by reminding the Galatian congregation, that his mission to the Gentile churches did not come from some church leader, but came directly from the risen

Christ (Gal. 1:11-17). He makes this assertion even in the title that he uses in this letter, which is unique among his correspondence (Gal. 1:1). He then further notes that not only is the gospel that he is teaching of divine origin but that he met with the leaders of the Jerusalem church during the apostolic council, and they endorsed Paul's mission to the Gentile churches. He then uses Titus as a case study. Titus, an uncircumcised Gentile, accompanied Paul to the apostolic council. If that council had believed what these Jewish Christian missionaries have been teaching the Galatian congregations, that Gentile Christians must be circumcised, they would have insisted on circumcising Titus who was acting as a prophet and teacher to the church in Antioch (Gal. 2:3). But they did nothing of the sort. Paul strongly advocates a sense of equality between the circumcised and uncircumcised believers arguing that neither should feel superior in any way to the other.

Paul then continues to make his case by emphasizing how Jewish he actually was before his conversion. Based on his background, if

any Christian should act Jewish, it would be
Paul. But Paul highlights the fact that working
under the law is a curse, makes one a slave and
is equivalent to idolatry. He does not wish
slavery for his fellow Christians in Galatia, but
wishes freedom that comes through life "in
Christ."

While Paul was wrapping up his time in
Ephesus, he both received word from Chloe's
people concerning the situation in Corinth and
a letter that the Corinthians had written him.
With the Corinthians, Paul takes a different approach than the one he had used with the Galatians. Apollo had been preaching in Corinth
for a few years at that point, but he does not
lay any of the blame on the missionaries, but
rather takes the church members themselves to
task. This letter talks a fantastic deal about the
Corinthians forming parties amongst themselves (I Cor. 1:11ff.) and about "strong people" (I Cor. 6:12; 10:23). The Corinthian
Christians were convinced they possessed divine wisdom and placed much emphasis on the
wisdom sayings of Jesus. In this way, they had

transformed the Christian gospel message into a type of mystery cult.

Paul, therefore, combats this tendency and highlights the areas where the gospel message most contrasts with the mystery cults. He stresses that he and Apollos are both servants of Christ and not the vessels for wise insights into the divine realm. Being Christians does not convey any supernatural rights or special privileges, but on the contrary, Christ crucified is a stumbling-block and foolishness. This sense of privilege seems to have spilled over into various aspects of these Christians lives. Some of the Corinthian Christians believed they had the right to have sex with prostitutes. Others refused sex in marriage or rejected marriage outright. Another group promoted living together in spiritual marriages. Just as Paul promoted equality between circumcised and uncircumcised believers when writing to the Galatians, writing to the Corinthians he promotes equality between women and men in the marriage relationship (I Cor. 7:3-4).

Paul moves from the general topic of marriage to eating food sacrificed to idols, where this sense of privilege still persists. Paul grants that the Christian possesses both freedom and privilege but that they should renounce it out of respect for the weak consciences of others in the congregation. Paul holds himself out as an example noting that he has renounced his own privileges for the gospel's sake. Paul finally addresses the denial of the resurrection by several members of the Corinthian congregation. Paul situates the resurrection as an actual event that will take place at a moment in time as opposed to a timeless truth like the immortality of the soul. Paul concludes by informing Corinth about the collection he has started for the Jerusalem church and his plans to bring it there.

Paul's overall approach to the problems that have arisen in the Corinthian community was not to set out a certain code of rules and minimum standards that must be met. He instead tried to identify governing principles that the church leaders could use to evaluate and proscribe conduct even as new situations arise.

Once Paul thought he had addressed the issues in Corinth another set of problems ap-

peared. Similar to what took place in Galatia
several months prior, Jewish Christian missionaries came to Corinth boasting of their Jewish
lineage. According to these missionaries, the
Christian message was the renewal of true Ju-
daism. Rather than focusing on the Torah or
circumcision, these missionaries focused on the
ability to perform miracles and spiritual inter-
pretation of the scriptures and their own mysti-
cal experiences. The appearance of this group
in Corinth prompted Paul to both change his
travel plans and to write a third letter to the
Corinthians (II Corinthians 2:14-6:13; 7:2-4).

It is vital to note here that despite its appearance in modern English Bibles, the epistle
designated II Corinthians is actually a combination of several different letters that Paul wrote
to the Corinthian church. They are all authentic
letters from Paul, but were written at different
times to address different circumstances.

These missionaries focused their preaching
on the miracles performed by Jesus and presented themselves to the Corinthian congregation with letters of recommendation that
mentioned their own powerful deeds and past

missionary successes. Paul's response to these missionaries is that the church is his heavenly letter written on their hearts.

This letter did not go over with the Corinthian congregation anywhere as well as his first second letter (I Corinthians) did. When news reached Paul that his letter had fallen flat, he picked up and took the next available ship to Corinth. This proved to be a bad move on Paul's part. The Corinthian congregation defied his authority brazenly, and one individual so offended him that he left Corinth in a hurry emotionally battered.

Not one to be easily dissuaded, when Paul arrived in Ephesus again, he sat down to write another letter (II Corinthians 10-13). Here, Paul uses his rhetorical training to its fullest employing everything from threats to irony and satire. This letter serves as an apology for his entire mission to the Gentiles. He takes on the super-apostles and mocks every aspect of their persona. He also notes that he would be forced to dissolve the congregation at Corinth to the best of his ability if this conflict cannot be resolved. He then handed the letter to Titus to try to salvage the relationship between apostle and the congregation he founded.

Although Luke does not mention any imprisonment of Paul in Ephesus, the later correspondence Paul will have with Corinth (II Corinthians 1:1-2:13; 7:5-16) makes reference to prison and fearing a death sentence (II Cor. 1:8-11). It was while he was in prison at Ephesus that Paul received a welcome visit from his friend Epaphroditus who came bearing gifts from the Philippian congregation. Unfortunately, he became sick while he was with Paul. Once Epaphroditus recovered, Paul sent him back to Philippi along with a letter to the Philippian congregation. The theme of the letter was courage in the face of harsh circumstances, even death. This letter contains a hymn-like passage (2:6-11) that was likely already part of the early church tradition where Christ becomes the model of such unassailable courage.

Onesimus the runaway slave Paul had met a year or so earlier visited Paul in prison where he convinced Onesimus to return to Philemon. Paul agreed to write a letter on Onesimus' behalf in an attempt to soften the blow that

would inevitably come as the result of a runaway slave returning to his master. Rather than
writing a private letter to Onesimus, as he certainly could have done, he writes an open letter
hoping that airing the situation will be the best
way to save Onesimus from the severest forms
of punishment he might receive (Philemon 1:1).
Paul highlights how helpful Onesimus has been
in his missionary work in Ephesus suggesting
that Onesimus would be helpful to Philemon
too. Paul, although in prison himself, offers to
pay any expenses that Onesimus may owe (Philemon 18-19).

Once Paul was released from prison, his first
priority was to repair his damaged relationship
with the Corinthian congregation. This meant
that he changed his travel plans again. Paul
sent Titus ahead of him to Corinth, while Paul
and Timothy went to Troas. They waited for
Titus in Troas, but when he didn't show, they
continued on to Philippi (Macedonia). Titus
met the two of them in Macedonia carrying the
news that the Corinthians had forgiven Paul
and were willing to restore their relationship
with him. With this news Paul wrote another

letter to the Corinthian congregation (II Cor. 1:1-2:13; 7:5-16). Paul tells the Corinthians about his afflictions in prison in Ephesus and God's comfort through the midst of those trials. He also asks the congregation to ensure that the individual with whom he had the row be reconciled with both himself and the congregation, as well. He also notes that being released from prison did not end his affliction, but rather hearing Titus' recent report brought an end to his affliction.

He then sent two letters concerning the Jerusalem collection, with one to Corinth (II Cor. 8) and the other to Achaea (II Cor. 9). With these letters completed, the collection would finally be complete, and he could deliver it to Jerusalem and make good on the commitment he made at the Apostolic Council.

It is crucial to note at this point that the Eastern Syriac churches include in their canon a text designated III Corinthians. This text is clearly pseudonymous and was written to address theological disputes in the second century CE.

Paul followed up his letter asking for dona-
tions for the poor in the Jerusalem congregation with a visit to Corinth to reunite with his
congregation and to collect whatever money
they had raised. After Paul had reconciled with
the Corinthians and had completed the collection for Jerusalem, he wrote his letter to the
Romans. For whatever reason, it appears that
Paul produced two copies of this letter. One
copy that included chapters 1-15, he sent to
Rome, while the other copy, which included
chapters 1-16 he sent to Ephesus. Chapter 16
is essentially a letter of recommendation for
Phoebe.

This was the last letter that Paul wrote, and
his theology is fully developed. He deals with
some of the themes that he has touched on in
various ways in previous letters, but because
this letter is written to a church he has already
planted that has particular issues to sort out,
Paul's thought is more programmatic and complete in this letter. It seems that Paul wrote
Romans with the operating assumption that
this is what he would want to tell the church if
he were for some reason unable to make it

there in person. He talks of the gospel as the power of salvation for all. He emphasizes God's saving righteousness and justification by faith and the equality between circumcised and uncircumcised believers. He discusses life in Christ and rehearses the universal history of redemption. He closes by reviewing God's plan for the Jewish nation (Rom. 9-11)

[4]

LATER CAREER AND DEATH

Paul had initially planned to go straight to Rome from Corinth, allowing the collection to be delivered by trustworthy delegates from each of the churches who contributed to the funds (Rom. 15:22-24), but he was concerned about the safety of delivering this much money given the hostility posed by nonbelievers in Judea. Paul traveled with the delegates by boat where some Jews onboard tried to kill him. They escaped and took the land route instead from Corinth to Macedonia. From Philippi, they took a boat they made multiple stops before finally landing in Caesarea Palestine, the closest port city to Jerusalem. While in Jerusalem Paul visited the temple accompanied by his delegates from the Diaspora churches. While in the temple, someone recognized Paul and accused him of bringing a Gentile into the temple. Roman soldiers were called in to deal with the ruckus that ensued and Paul was arrested.

According to Luke, Paul was tried first before the Jewish Sanhedrin in Jerusalem (Acts 22:1-21), then, he narrowly escaped a plot on his life as they transported him to Caesarea Palestine escalating his case up to the governor Felix (Acts 23:12-35). Paul was held in prison for two years with little movement on his case.

After waiting for two years for the authorities to make a decision, he had been in prison long to see turnover in the state office. Festus became the new governor, replacing the old governor Felix (Acts 24:27). When Festus was brought up to speed on the charges Paul was facing, he offered Paul the opportunity to be tried in Jerusalem (Acts 25:9). Paul believed that his best chance was before the emperor's tribunal in Rome and filed a formal appeal with the court (Acts 25:10-12). Festus was more than happy to get rid of this prisoner and filed the necessary paperwork to send Paul to Rome. The interlude about King Agrippa II (Acts 25:13-26:32) makes little sense from an historical standpoint. Governors and kings do not hear cases on which they do not plan on making a decision.

Paul's journey to Rome, on the other hand, is narrated in Acts by a "we passage." Koester dismisses this passage as legendary because he cannot imagine who could have joined Paul on his journey to Rome. A solution to this riddle may lie in the Gentile who accompanied Paul into the temple. If this charge were historically accurate, it would be embarrassing for the early church because it would at least lend some credence to the charges against Paul. Paul's case may have been bound up with the Gentile delegate who entered the temple with Paul. If this were the case, it helps explain why Paul's journey to Rome was narrated with a "we passage" that contains so much detail that does little to advance Luke's literary agenda.

Paul befriends the centurion responsible for his well-being. They sailed from Caesarea Palestine to Sidon, then to Cilicia, Pamphylia and Myra. At Myra, they switched ships and sailed to Cnidus, Salmone and Fair Havens. After Fair Havens, their ship was battered endlessly by a strong storm, and they became lost at sea, desperately low on supplies. Having spent two weeks adrift at sea, the boat was marooned on the island of Malta. After several misadventures over the course of three months, the winter ended and the group sailed to several ports before making it to Rome.

In Rome Paul lived by himself with the soldier who was guarding him (Acts 28:16). He lived two years under house arrest, preaching the gospel to whoever would listen. It is at this point that Luke's account ends.

Clement of Alexandria made the following comments about Paul's death in a letter he wrote during the decade of the 90's CE. The relevant section reads as follows:

Let us set before our eyes the good apostles...Because of jealousy and strife Paul showed the way to win the prize of endurance.

Seven times he was in bonds, he was driven away as an exile, he was a herald both in East and West, he won the noble glory of his faith. He taught righteousness to all the world, and when he had reached the limit of the West he gave his testimony before rulers, and thus passed from the world and was taken up into the Holy Place, the greatest example of endurance. (1 Clem. 5:4-7)

The Acts of Paul and Thecla report the martyrdom of Paul in much more lengthy passage. Because translations of this story are not easily available for most readers, a lengthy paraphrase of this story follows. It begins with a description of Paul buying a barn in Rome where he would preach to the people. One day, the cupbearer of the emperor, Patroclus, came to the barn to hear Paul preach. The barn was filled with people listening to Paul's preaching, so Patroclus sat in the upper window listening and dozing off slightly in the heat of the day fell from the window and died. A report of Patroclus' death immediately reached Emperor Nero's ears. Paul learned of it and asked for the crowd to go outside and find the boy who had fallen and bring him inside. The assembly lamented and mourned to Jesus in an attempt to appeal to Jesus to revive the boy to life. Their appeal worked, and the boy was restored to life and they sent him away on an equid of some kind.

While Nero climbed out of his bath, he was still grieving the death of Patroclus as he reluctantly told the attendant who accompanied him to appoint someone else as a wine-taster. Nero was not prepared for the reply that his attendant gave him, "Emperor, Patroclus is alive and stands at the sideboard." Fear gripped him, and it took him quite some time to enter the kitchen where this ghost was supposed to be standing. He finally mustered the courage and entered the kitchen, whereupon he immediately asked Patroclus to clarify whether he was yet alive or whether the figure standing before him was an apparition. As soon as Patroclus clarified that he was indeed alive, Nero inquired as to the source of his remarkable resurrection.

Patroclus was more than pleased to announce to Nero that it was "Christ Jesus, the

King of the Ages" who was to thank for his miraculous recovery. Just as the gospel stories of Jesus' crucifixion indicate that the imperial title "King of the Jews" was what got Jesus in trouble with the Roman authorities, so here, the later Christian writer telling the story of Paul's death imagined that it was the phrase "King of the ages" found in one of the Pastoral epistles attributed to Paul (I Tim. 1:17) that got him into trouble with Nero.

The mention of another king was one sure way to get Nero's hackles up. Nero predictably inquired further about this king. If his title is "King of the ages," does that mean that he plans to destroy all other kingdoms. And Patroclus, portrayed by the storyteller as an ecstatic new convert, completely oblivious to the double entendre embedded within the conversation, excitedly answered Nero thinking that this was his opportunity to evangelize to the king, "Yes, he destroys all kingdoms under heaven...and there will be no kingdom which escapes him." At this point, Nero was nearly beside himself at these blatant references to treason that were coming from the lips of his loyal servant. He tried once more to clarify that he was not mishearing his servant and asked Patroclus if he was fighting for this other king. Continuing to play the hapless sap, Patroclus answered Nero confidently that of course, he fights in the service of that king because it was that king who was responsible for raising him from the dead. But just when the situation couldn't get any worse, three of Nero's bodyguards who had been overhearing the conversation and were just as clueless as Patroclus about its implications chimed in acknowledging their shared allegiance in fighting for this "King of the ages".

Nero had heard enough and had the men both tortured and locked up in prison. Sensing that this treasonous rebellion was widespread, Nero instructed his men to find all those who acknowledged being soldiers of this "King of the ages" and to summarily execute them. His men carried out this order, which resulted in the arrest of the apostle Paul. Those Christians who were collected in the same prison cell naturally looked to Paul as their leader, which did not go unnoticed by Nero. He pulled Paul aside demanding an explanation for this act of sedition. In a manner clearly uncharacteristic of the historical picture of Paul that has emerged above, who was hypersensitive to the life situation of every audience he addressed and modified his message accordingly, Paul himself preaches to Nero as if he is unfazed by the natural meaning of his words. He describes to the emperor his extensive recruitment program for inducting soldiers into this king's army. He then has the audacity to ask Caesar Nero to bow down and submit to this other king, followed by what reads as a veiled threat that this other king will destroy the world in its entirety in a single day. Paul clearly did nothing to mitigate Nero's anger and only managed to incite it further. Nero passed his sentence immediately declaring that Paul should be beheaded while the other "soldiers of the King of the ages" whom he had recruited were to be burned.

Paul continued to preach to a Roman official named Longus and a soldier named Cestus. As Nero's executioners proceeded to carry out some of these sentences, the Romans took notice and respectfully appealed to Nero noting that executing Roman soldiers without trial was only managing to weaken his own position. Struck by the wisdom of the objection, Nero changed his position to require that no Christian could be tortured or executed without a formal trial of their case first. So after this change in position, Paul appeared before Nero a second time and Nero again demanded Paul be executed. Rather than seeking to defend himself, Paul threatened Nero that were he executed, he would rise from the dead and appear before him paralleling what Patroclus had done earlier in the story.

Back in prison Paul continued to preach to Longus and Cestus. They both desired the salvation of which Paul preached, so they offered to release Paul if he would help them to be saved. But Paul steadfastly refused to allow them to release him from prison and was dead set on facing his punishment head on (or off, as the case might be). While they were speaking two other guards came to check on Paul's status and Paul pulled them aside to preach to them, as well. They dismissed Paul's claims stating that they would believe only after they saw Paul risen from the dead. When they left he returned his attention to Longus and Cestus and gave them further instruction as to where they could find him alongside Titus and Luke after he had been raised from the dead.

The executioner then led Paul away and beheaded him only to see milk spurting from his veins rather than blood. The Christian storyteller was probably thinking of the analogy Paul used with the Corinthian congregation when he compared his teaching of the gospel message to them as milk, as opposed to solid food (I Cor. 3:2). That same day when Nero was meeting with several philosophers and soldiers, the risen Paul (or the way the story reads it sounds more like the ghost of Paul) appeared to Nero affirming that he was yet alive. He then uttered a curse to Nero for his treatment of the Christians. Here again, although Paul clearly wishes his opponents in the Galatian congregation ill, there is no evidence of him uttering curses to even his arch-nemeses. The tale concludes with Titus and Luke baptizing Longus and Cestus after they followed Paul's instructions and had seen his ghost beside Titus and Luke when they had been praying earlier.

This tale concerning Paul's death is clearly filled with legendary material. Paul never describes Jesus as a king, though this theme does develop in the Pastoral Epistles and the gospels, both written a decade or two after Paul's death. The theme is Christians as soldiers of Christ is later still and dates to the second century at the earliest. At its core, though, is likely historical information that Paul was among the Christians martyred by Nero. It is more likely, however, that he was simply treated by the Romans as one Christian among many and that his death occurred alongside that of many other Christians who were killed at the same time.

CONCLUSION

Paul of Tarsus, the apostle to the Gentiles, was responsible for shaping so much of early Christian theology and politics that the importance of his life can hardly be overestimated.

He had a quiet strength about him that allowed him to fulfill several personal commitments that lasted over many years, including his Nazirite vow and the collection for the poor in Jerusalem.

He had a sharp mind, that despite minimal formal education, he was able to navigate complex theological and philosophical questions with ease. He was passionate about his religious convictions both before and after his conversion experience. He was clearly mindful of the situations in which those with whom he communicated found themselves and always met them emotionally and spiritually in that place.

It seems that he firmly believed that the risen Christ had met him in his own situation, where he was as he says of himself "one untimely born" (I Cor. 15:8), and he sought to do for others that which Christ had done for him.

BIBLIOGRAPHY

Borg, Marcus J. and John Dominic Crossan. The First Paul: Reclaiming the Radical

Vissionary Behind the Church's Conservative Icon. New York, 2009.

Bornkamm, Günther. Paul. New York, 1971.

Chilton, Bruce D. and Jacob Neusner. "Paul and Gamaliel." Bulletin for Biblical

Research 14 (2004) 1-43.

Drane, John. Introducing the New Testament. Cambridge, 1986.

Elliott, J. K. The Apocryphal New Testament: A Collection of Apocryphal Christian

Literature in an English Translation. Oxford, 1993.

Kee, Howard Clark. Understanding the New Testament. 4th ed. New Jersey, 1983.

Knox, John. Chapters in the Life of Paul. New York, 1946.

Koester, Helmut. Introduction to the New Testament. 2 Vols. New York, 1982.

Stott, John R. W. The Message of Acts. Leicester, 1990.

Made in the USA
Columbia, SC
29 November 2022

72267945R00048